Valentine Be Mine

WITHDRAWN

Jacqueline Farmer

Illustrated by
Megan Halsey
and
Sean Addy

Charlesbridge

February 14 is Valentine's Day! On this holiday people show love and affection for their friends, family, and loved ones.

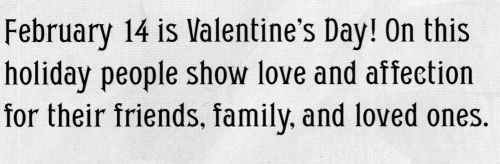

Today Valentine's Day is a romantic and love-filled holiday celebrated around the world. Sweethearts give each other flowers, candy, and gifts. Some couples share candlelit dinners. Schoolchildren decorate mailboxes to hold cards received from teachers and classmates. They play games and enjoy cookies and heart-shaped candies.

Valentine's Day's origins can be found in ancient Rome, but the holiday has changed a lot over the centuries. Religious customs, poets and kings, and hearts and flowers are all part of the story.

Ti amo.
Je t'aime.
Te amo.
I love you.

Love doesn't make
the world go 'round;
love is what makes
the ride worthwhile.
Franklin P. Jones

The holiday gets its name from three religious figures named Valentine. One was a priest who rebelled against a Roman emperor.

In the late first century, Valentine was a popular name. It came from the word *valens,* which meant "admirable." So it's no surprise that at least three religious men named Valentine lived during this period.

One Valentine was a priest in Rome. In the second century the Roman Empire was growing rapidly. Emperor Claudius II needed lots of soldiers to protect his distant lands. When he discovered that married men did not want to go to war, he banned all weddings. Dismayed, Valentine continued to marry people in secret. Claudius put Valentine in jail and tried, without success, to make him reject his Christian faith.

Legend says that while imprisoned, Valentine restored the sight of his jailor's blind daughter. When the girl's grateful family converted to Christianity, Claudius was outraged. He ordered Valentine executed on February 14. On the eve of his execution, the priest sent the girl a note signed "From your Valentine."

Love is the joy of the good, the wonder of the wise, the amazement of the gods.

Plato

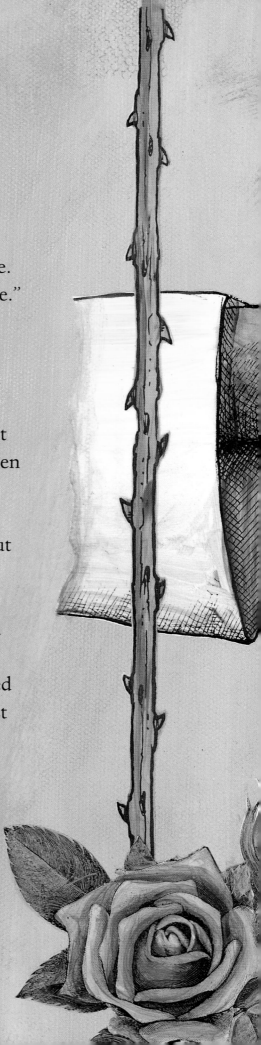

Another Valentine was a bishop, and yet another was a missionary. All three Valentines died on February 14.

According to legend, Valentine the Bishop of Terni lived at the same time as Valentine of Rome. The bishop cured a boy of "falling sickness," a crippling disease that is now called epilepsy. When witnesses to the miracle converted to Christianity, angry Roman senators arrested Bishop Valentine.

A third Valentine, a priest, was killed while a missionary in Africa. Little is known of his works.

All three Valentines were martyred, or killed for their beliefs, on February 14 and were later declared saints by the church. In their honor the holiday is called Saint Valentine's Day.

Love conquers all.

Virgil

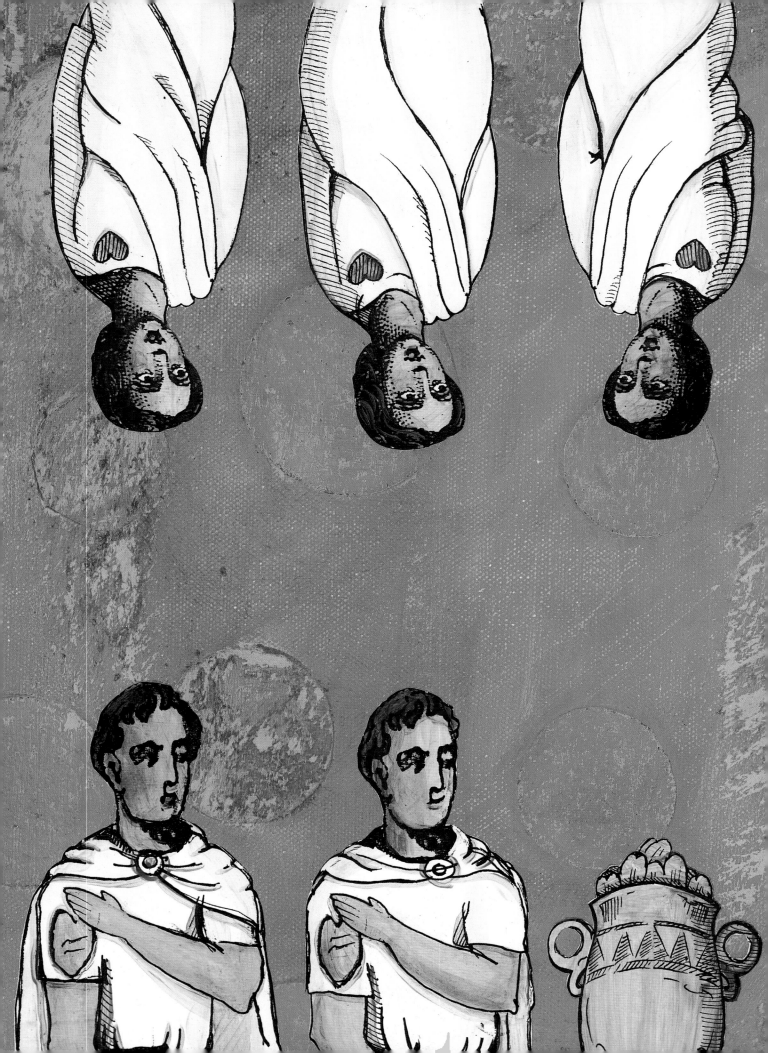

Many people believe the romantic traditions of Valentine's Day come from an ancient Roman holiday.

Before the start of the Roman Empire, Romans celebrated a fertility festival called *Lupercalia* (loo-per-CAHL-ee-ah). Not much is known about how this holiday was observed.

According to one Lupercalia legend, though, women would put signed love notes in a jug. Young men would remove a note from the jug and pin the chosen girl's name to their sleeves. They were then expected to protect that girl until the next festival.

Scholars once believed Lupercalia's fertility and marriage customs were connected to Valentine's Day. Recent research says otherwise. In AD 496, Pope Gelasius proclaimed February 14 the Feast of Saint Valentine to honor the martyred saints. He also ordered the Roman senate to abolish Lupercalia. This convinced scholars that the feast day had nothing to do with lovers, romance, or fertility and was strictly a Christian holiday.

Love is the greatest refreshment in life.
Pablo Picasso

Thanks to a poet and a royal marriage, Valentine's Day became a holiday about love and romance.

One of the first historical links of Valentine's Day to romance can be found in the writings of the famous English poet Geoffrey Chaucer.

In 1381 Chaucer wrote "The Parlement of Foules" (a.k.a. "The Parliament of Birds"), a poem to honor the engagement of King Richard II of England and Anne of Bohemia. The poem associated the mating season of birds with Saint Valentine's Day, changing a religious holiday into one that celebrated love:

For this was on seynt Valentines day,
When euery bryd comyth
there chese his make . . .

At the touch
of love everyone
becomes a poet.
Plato

For this was on
Saint Valentine's Day,
When every bird came
there to choose his mate . . .

A few years later, on February 14, 1400,
a High Court of Love was established in Paris.
The court was responsible for dealing with all
matters of love, including betrayals and love
contracts to protect the bride's and groom's rights.

A duke in captivity may have started the tradition of sending valentines.

Charles, Duke of Orleans, a young French nobleman, often gets the credit for writing one of the first valentines. After the battle at Agincourt, Charles was imprisoned in the Tower of London. During his twenty-five years of captivity (1415–1440), he wrote numerous love poems, some of which are on display in the British Museum. These poems may be the earliest surviving valentines.

By the sixteenth century, handwritten valentines were popular. In 1723 books called "valentine writers" provided romantics with love poems and sentimental ideas to be used in creating cards. It wasn't until the mid-1800s that fancy cards, decorated with ribbons and lace, became popular.

The best and most beautiful things in the world cannot be seen nor even touched but just felt in the heart.

Helen Keller

about the weary tower has la
ter, and ruin laid
ome store of pleasure give me a
with all them of his part
e about the weary tower has la
break his bands thou art afra
to make his cruel force depart
at least this castle of my hear
ome store of pleasure give me a
t not Jealousy, for all his art
r, and the tower in ruin laid

In the nineteenth century, Valentine's Day cards became big business. In Massachusetts a woman named Esther Howland sold beautiful handmade cards.

After receiving an English valentine, Esther Howland tried her hand at making her own. She bought paper lace and floral decorations from England and used designs from European cards as her guide. Her cards became so popular that she needed to find a faster way to make them.

Ms. Howland called upon her female friends and hired other workers through an ad in a Worcester newspaper. She set up an assembly line in her home, and her sales grew. Eventually, she even sent kits to workers who assembled cards in their homes.

Creative and smart, Ms. Howland designed two original valentine cards. One used brightly colored tissue under paper lace to show off the intricate design. She also produced shadow-box cards, which had a three-dimensional look.

Called the "Mother of the American Valentine," Ms. Howland sold her cards for between five cents and fifty dollars each. Soon she was earning up to $100,000 a year!

The more I give to thee, the more I have; for both are infinite.
William Shakespeare

Anyone can make a sweet valentine for that special someone.

To make a Mouse of Hearts Valentine's Day card you'll need:
- 1 sheet gray construction paper
- 1 sheet pink construction paper
- crayons
- tape
- tiny lollipop or a piece of string licorice

1. Fold the gray paper in half.
2. Draw half a heart along the fold.
3. Cut along the line you have drawn. Keep the heart folded; this is the mouse's body—the point is its nose. Cut two small hearts for the mouse's ears out of the pink paper.
4. Tape the pink hearts on each side of the mouse's head.
5. Use a crayon to draw the eyes and whiskers.
6. Open the gray paper heart and write a note, such as "Be my squeakie!"
7. Refold the heart and tape it together along the back, leaving enough room at the V of the heart to insert the candy. If using a lollipop, leave the stick showing as a tail. If using string licorice, secure the candy with tape so it won't fall out of the card.

This sweetie treat is sure to please.

How do I love thee?
Let me count the ways.
Elizabeth Barrett Browning

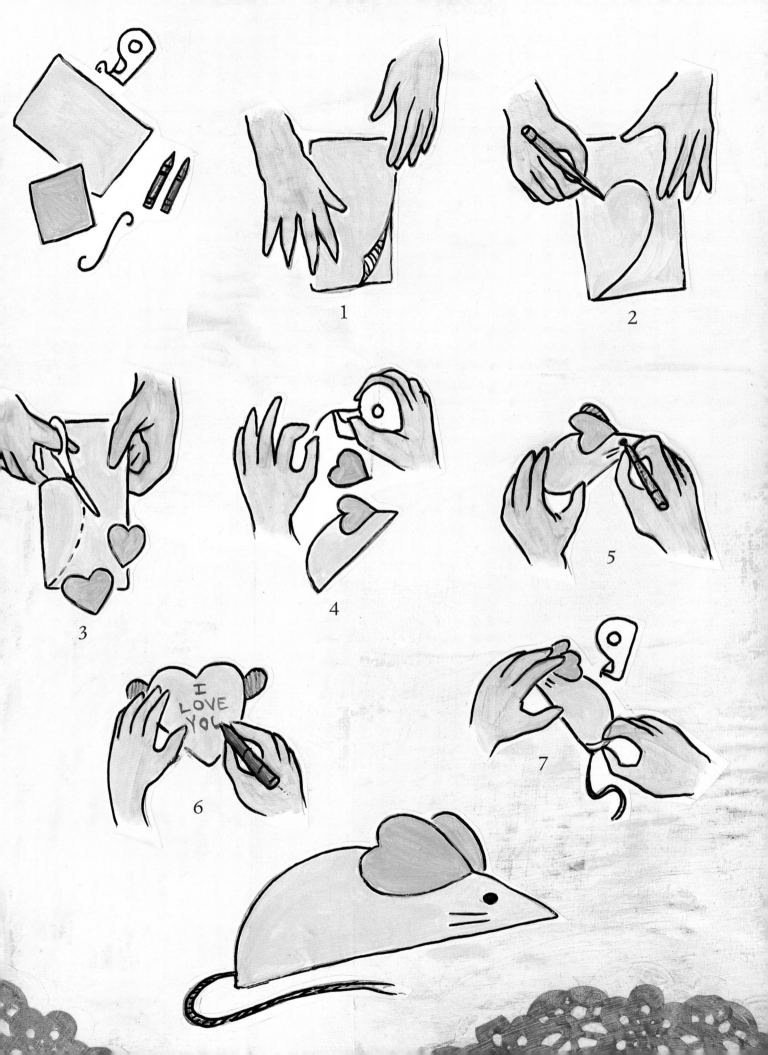

1

2

3

4

5

6

7

Lots of symbols are associated with Valentine's Day. Cupid and doves are two of the oldest.

Cupid, the god of love, may be the most famous symbol of Valentine's Day. According to Roman mythology he would shoot invisible, painless arrows into people, making them fall instantly in love with the next person they saw. Shown as either a chubby, happy child with wings or a handsome young man, Cupid has become a symbol of playful love.

Doves have represented love and peace for thousands of years. Cupid's mother, Venus, the goddess of love, drove a chariot drawn by doves. Geoffrey Chaucer wrote poems about doves mating for life. And according to the Holy Bible, the dove is the symbol of the Holy Spirit.

Cupid and doves are often used on Valentine's Day cards and in holiday decorations to portray romantic or spiritual love.

Being deeply loved by someone gives you strength, while loving someone deeply gives you courage.

Lao Tzu

Hearts are a symbol of true love.

Long ago, people believed that feelings, such as love, anger, and fear, were hidden in the heart. So giving your heart to your lover meant giving your whole being.

Today the heart is seen as the symbolic home of love. The colors of hearts are symbolic, too. Red hearts represent passionate love, while pink ones stand for romance.

At Valentine's Day celebrations, it is common to see heart-shaped cards, balloons, cakes, candies, and even chocolate boxes. Stores stock up on fancy, chocolate-filled, heart-shaped boxes for the holiday, making chocolate the sweetest symbol of Valentine's Day.

Many cultures have considered chocolate to be a gift from the gods. In ancient Mexico the Aztecs and Maya believed that the cacao bean, which is used to make chocolate, had spiritual qualities. Today chocolate is considered an energy booster. It's also said to contain a chemical that makes people feel as if they are in love. Maybe this is why chocolate is a favorite treat among lovers.

Age does not protect you from love. But love, to some extent, protects you from age.

Jeanne Moreau

People often send flowers to say, "I love you!"

Gifts of flowers please men and women alike. Beautiful blossoms stir the senses with their fragrance, color, and variety. Red roses were the favorite flower of Venus. A symbol of love and passion, red roses are sent by the millions as Valentine's Day gifts to sweethearts and dear friends around the world.

A "floral lexicon" is a flower dictionary: it provides a special meaning for every flower. Here are just a few:

- ♥ red roses: I love you passionately.
- ♥ calla lily: You are exceptionally beautiful.
- ♥ gardenia: I love you secretly.
- ♥ lily of the valley: Let's make up.
- ♥ narcissus: Stay as sweet as you are.
- ♥ snapdragon: You are strong.
- ♥ red carnation: My heart aches for you.
- ♥ primrose: I cannot live without you.
- ♥ violet: I love you faithfully.

> If I had a flower for every time I thought of you, I could walk in my garden forever.
>
> Alfred Lord Tennyson

Just by choosing certain flowers, lovers can send secret messages to their sweeties! A bouquet of calla lilies, red roses, and primroses is a real winner. Or, as a desperate plea, try red carnations, primroses, and lilies of the valley. There's a flower to suit every occasion.

Tissue paper flowers can send a message, too—one that lasts a lifetime!

To make Valentine's Day tissue paper flowers you'll need:
    pieces of colored tissue, each piece should measure
        about 8 x 12 inches
    1 pipe cleaner
    green crepe paper cut into 24-inch strips
    1 green bamboo garden stick
    sturdy tape

1. Make a neat pile of tissue pieces.
2. Fold the paper stack accordion style.
3. Twist a pipe cleaner tightly around the center of the folded tissue.
4. Round each tissue end with scissors.
5. Gently separate the tissue layers by pulling them up and toward the center one at a time until they look like flower petals.
6. Twist two strips of crepe paper around the pipe cleaner at the base of the flower.
7. Then twist the rest of the pipe cleaner and flower to the bamboo stick and secure it with sturdy tape.

This is a lovely gift for a special person—like Mom, perhaps?

Love is like a butterfly. It goes wherever it pleases, and it pleases wherever it goes.

Unknown

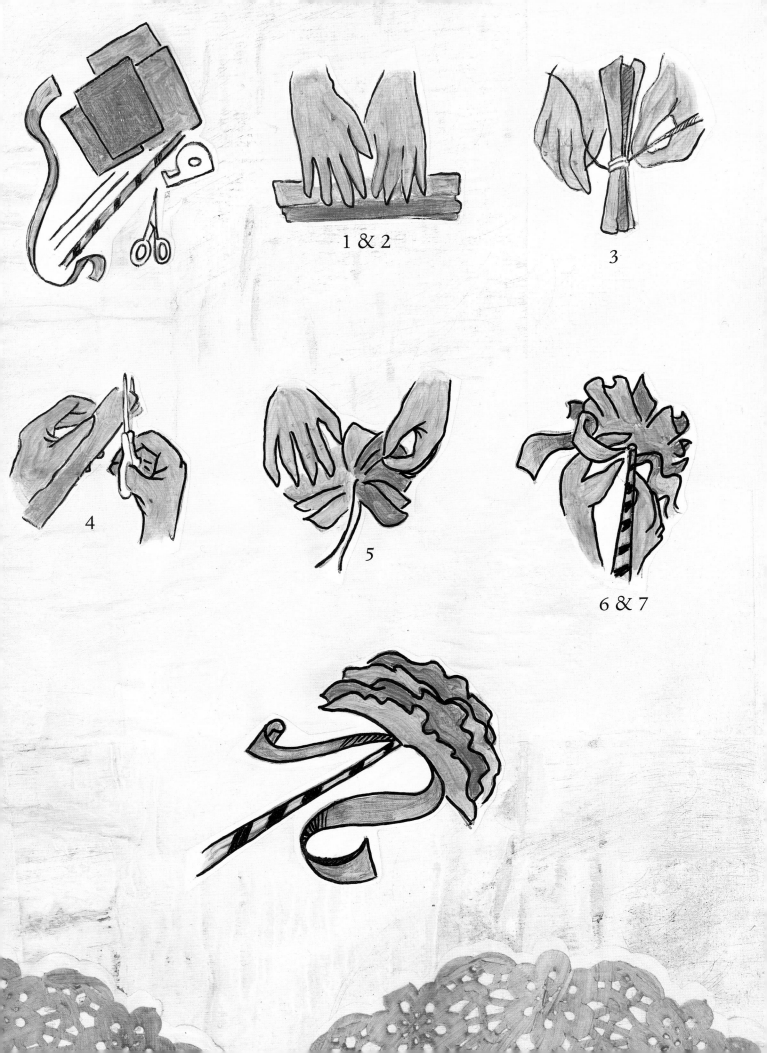

1 & 2

3

4

5

6 & 7

Valentine traditions are unique around the world. People from Great Britain celebrate with music and literature, while Italians enjoy fine foods and gifts.

In Great Britain children sing Valentine's Day songs. Parents and teachers reward their efforts with fruit or money.

Geoffrey Chaucer would be pleased to find that British men and women still carry on the tradition he started hundreds of years ago. They compose romantic love poems, the best of which are published in newspapers.

In Italy lovers give perfume and jewelry along with chocolate and flowers to their sweethearts. A traditional gift is a *baci perugina* (BAH-chee peh-roo-GEE-nah), a small chocolate-covered hazelnut. Like a Chinese fortune cookie, the candy is wrapped in a note—often a romantic quote, written in four languages!

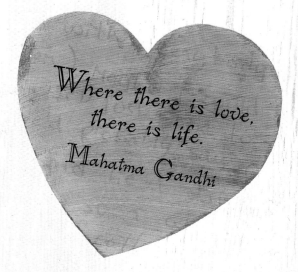

Danes have a funny way to celebrate their valentines, while the Japanese get serious about chocolate.

Danish men write romantic mystery letters called *gaekkebrev* (gah-kee-BREF). Known as "joking letters," they are signed only with dots . . . one dot for each letter in the writer's name. Ladies who guess the name of their mysterious lover are rewarded with decorated eggs at Easter time.

The most popular gift in Denmark is a "lover's card." Long ago these were transparent cards that, when backlit, revealed a picture of the lover presenting a small gift. Today any card with a loving note is a "lover's card." A favorite small gift is a pressed white flower called a snowdrop.

Japanese traditions favor gifts of chocolate. On Valentine's Day a Japanese woman gives chocolates, called *honmei choco* (HOHN-may CHOH-koh), to the man she loves. On March 14 the man who received the chocolates returns the favor by giving chocolates to the woman who gifted them to him the month before.

Chocolates are also given as a gesture of respect for bosses and coworkers. These gifts are called *giri choco* (gee-RREE CHOH-koh), or "obligation chocolates."

To love is to receive a glimpse
of heaven.
Karen Sunde

At the end of the day, everyone can be a valentine—a funny valentine, that is!

Valentine Jokes

♥ **Q**: What did the elephant say to his girlfriend?
♥ **A**: I love you a ton!

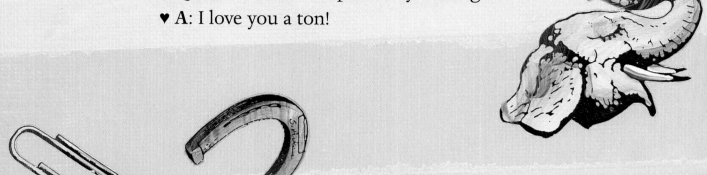

♥ **Q**: What did the paper clip say to the magnet?
♥ **A**: I find you very attractive.

♥ **Q**: What kind of flower do you never give on Valentine's Day?
♥ **A**: Cauliflower!

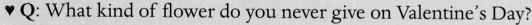

♥ **Q**: Did you hear about the nearsighted porcupine?
♥ **A**: He fell in love with a pincushion!

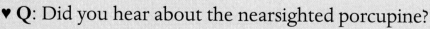

♥ **Q**: What did the chocolate syrup say to the ice cream?
♥ **A**: I'm sweet on you!

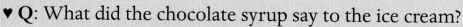

Valentine's Day is a perfect time to say, "You're special,"
"I think you're cute," or "I love you" to friends, family, and
loved ones. Cards, candy, flowers—even tissue paper flowers—
can send a loving message. But a gift isn't necessary. A sweet
hug or kiss will do nicely, and neither costs a thing! After all,
Valentine's Day is a good time to give the gift of love.

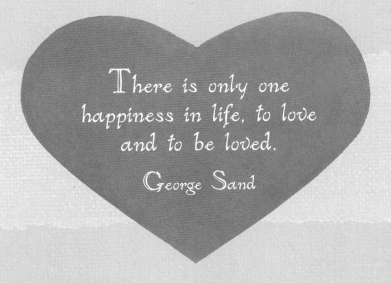

There is only one
happiness in life, to love
and to be loved.
George Sand

Did you know . . .

- ♥ A common valentine's card signature is XOXOXO. Each X represents a kiss. Each O represents a hug.
- ♥ According to history.com, 141,000,000 Valentine's Day cards are exchanged in the United States each year. This number is second only to the number of cards sent at Christmas.
- ♥ About 3 percent of pet owners will give Valentine's Day gifts to their pets.

♥ The village of St. Valentin in Indre, France, takes Valentine's Day to the extreme. This lovely village celebrates with a three-day festival from February 12 to 14. Villagers decorate their houses and the town with flowers and hearts. Events include dinner, dancing, and fireworks. But tourists can visit year-round to experience the Lover's Garden, have their cards postmarked at the St. Valentin post office, buy a souvenir at the Valentin Kiosk, visit the Valentin House, and even post love notes on the Tree of Vows.

To my wonderful children, Brent and Christina. They make me proud.
—J. F.

For my first Valentine, the boy who still plays the guitar. XOXOXO
—M. H.

To my wife, Tonya. I have moved heaven to find you and will move earth to hold you.
And sit in wonderment at our children's beauty, for they are the perfect reflection of you.
—S. A.

Library of Congress Cataloging-in-Publication Data
Farmer, Jacqueline.
  Valentine be mine / Jacqueline Farmer ; illustrated by
Megan Halsey and Sean Addy.
    p. cm.
  ISBN 978-1-58089-389-3 (reinforced for library use)
  ISBN 978-1-58089-390-9 (softcover)
1. Valentine's Day—Juvenile literature. I. Title.
GT4925.F37 2013
394.2618—dc23   2011049504

Printed in China
(hc) 10 9 8 7 6 5 4 3 2 1
(sc) 10 9 8 7 6 5 4 3 2 1

Text copyright © 2013 by Jacqueline Farmer
Illustrations copyright © 2013 by Megan Halsey and Sean Addy

Published by Charlesbridge
85 Main Street
Watertown, MA 02472
(617) 926-0329
www.charlesbridge.com

Illustrations were created on canvas paper using mixed media collage:
  photographs, vintage clip-art, hand-drawn images, and acrylic paints
Display type set in Gable Antique by Spiece Graphics
Text type set in Dante MT by The Monotype Corporation plc
Color separations by KHL Chroma Graphics, Singapore
Manufactured by Regent Publishing Services, Hong Kong
Printed September 2012 in Shenzhen, Guangdong, China
Production supervision by Brian G. Walker
Designed by Diane M. Earley